THE NEW PSYCHOLOGY OF SALES PERFORMANCE

Why **POSITIVE, PERSEVERING, GRITTY** Extraverts
Will Transform Your Sales Force, and How To Find Them

TIMOTHY L. COOMER, PhD

BALBOA
PRESS
A DIVISION OF HAY HOUSE

Balboa Press books may be ordered through booksellers or by contacting:

Balboa Press
A Division of Hay House
1663 Liberty Drive
Bloomington, IN 47403
www.balboapress.com
1 (877) 407-4847

Because of the dynamic nature of the Internet, any web addresses or
links contained in this book may have changed since publication and
may no longer be valid. The views expressed in this work are solely those
of the author and do not necessarily reflect the views of the publisher,
and the publisher hereby disclaims any responsibility for them.

The author of this book does not dispense medical advice or prescribe the use
of any technique as a form of treatment for physical, emotional, or medical
problems without the advice of a physician, either directly or indirectly. The
intent of the author is only to offer information of a general nature to help
you in your quest for emotional and spiritual well-being. In the event you use
any of the information in this book for yourself, which is your constitutional
right, the author and the publisher assume no responsibility for your actions.

Any people depicted in stock imagery provided by Getty Images are
models, and such images are being used for illustrative purposes only.
Certain stock imagery © Getty Images.

Print information available on the last page.

ISBN: 978-1-9822-2789-0 (sc)
ISBN: 978-1-9822-2790-6 (e)

Library of Congress Control Number: 2019906852

Balboa Press rev. date: 05/09/2019

CONTENTS

1

INTRODUCTION

A few years ago, I had the opportunity to meet one of the insurance brokerage industry's most successful "producers" (the industry's term for salespeople). This man had generated millions of dollars in commissions for years, had been labeled a "power broker" by industry journals, and was managing one of the most successful regional offices for a national brokerage firm. We had become friends over the years as my business supported his successful sales efforts with actuarial services and analytical software.

As an entrepreneur, I was interested in understanding what this undisputed industry leader viewed as the main challenges in the insurance brokerage world. When I asked him that question, he paused briefly and then replied, "If you can figure out how to identify who will succeed as a salesperson, then you will have solved the biggest challenge this industry faces."

That was not the answer I expected, but it led me on a journey to understand the factors that contribute to sales performance. In fact, I entered a prestigious executive leadership program at Oklahoma State University so that I could examine this topic at the Ph.D. level. I approached this endeavor in the same way that I have approached all my high-level analytical work—seeking to do quality research and distill the results down to the practical level so as to benefit the sales profession.

Thanks to my established reputation and extensive contacts within the insurance field, I was able to access a research sample that few others could have secured. My pilot research had a sample of 1,200 respondents, and my detailed personality testing involved more than 150 insurance salespeople—with an average salary of $137,000—and their supervisors. In other words, I was able to test my hypotheses on the relationships between personality factors and sales performance with a sample of very successful professionals. I am deeply grateful to the salespeople who patiently answered nearly 150 questions each, as well as the supervisors who provided performance evaluations, so that my results could have a high degree of statistical reliability.

My findings have compelling, easy-to-apply implications for the all-important task of cultivating a productive sales force in any B2B setting. In this small booklet, I explain what I have learned and how you can put this information to work. I have tried to keep things short and simple. If you want more details, you can look up my whole dissertation online at https://shareok.org/handle/11244/48794. Or feel free to contact me with questions at TLC@ SIGMAactuary.com.

To help you understand my findings, first I need to take you through a brief primer on the relevant concepts of personality psychology. (If you are already familiar with the Big Five personality traits, HEXACO, grit, and PsyCap, you can skip the next chapter.) With this information in hand, you'll be able to readily understand my findings and how you can apply them.

2

UNDERSTANDING THE RELEVANT PERSONALITY FACTORS

The Big Five Personality Model

Ever since Sir Francis Galton's work in the 1880s, psychology researchers have been fascinated by the idea that by carefully studying our use of language, we could identify the main factors that make up human personality. By the 1960s, research settled on a five-factor model of personality, commonly known as the Big Five personality traits. Following is a brief explanation of the five factors.

Openness to Experience: This category describes people who are intellectual, creative, unconventional, imaginative, innovative, and philosophical. They tend to appreciate beauty in art and nature, are intellectually curious, use imagination in everyday life, and like to hear unusual opinions.

Emotionality: This trait, often referred to by the not-very-nice title of neuroticism, describes one's level of emotional stability. People with high levels of emotionality tend to be anxious, depressed, angry, embarrassed, emotional, worried, and insecure—obviously not desirable personality traits for most jobs.

Extraversion: Extraverts display expressiveness, social boldness, sociability, and liveliness. They are assertive, active, energetic, and adventurous. When people think about the characteristics of a successful salesperson—competitive, anxious to succeed by pleasing others—they usually think of traits represented by Extraversion.

Agreeableness: This trait encompasses forgiveness, gentleness, flexibility, and patience—all aspects of personality that are valuable in social interaction and customer service, though they have historically not been related with sales performance in previous research.

Conscientiousness: People high in this trait are very organized, work hard, and act responsibly. They are orderly with things and with time, highly concerned for accuracy and perfection, prudent, and careful decision makers. Whereas extraverts are motivated by rewards, conscientious people are intrinsically motivated to achieve their high goals for the sake of the accomplishment itself, for personal satisfaction, and because they believe it is the right way to do things. Conscientiousness is positively correlated with job performance in a broad spectrum of industries and especially in sales.

A Sixth Personality Factor Shows Up

This Big Five model has been widely used in personality research for decades, but more recent language analysis has suggested that there should be six factors. In 2004, Michael Ashton and Kibeom Lee proposed a six-factor structure, with **Honesty-Humility** as the new factor. People with this trait are sincere, honest, faithful, loyal, modest, unassuming, and ethical; they avoid manipulating others, are scrupulously fair, tend not to value wealth or luxury, and don't consider themselves superior to others.

Ashton and Lee's resulting six-factor model, which includes some alterations to two of the other factors, is known as **HEXACO**, for Honesty-Humility, Emotionality, eXtraversion, Agreeableness, Conscientiousness, and Openness to Experience.

Honesty-Humility has also been shown to be a predictor of job performance even when controlling for Conscientiousness; in other words, even when one compares people who are equally conscientious, the ones who are higher in Honesty-Humility perform better.

Grit

Grit is a relatively new construct (i.e., an aspect of behavior that we can describe but cannot directly observe) in personality psychology. It was developed by psychologist Angela Lee Duckworth, who has popularized her findings in the 2016 bestseller *Grit: The Power of Passion and Perseverance.*

Grit is about having the ability to push hard against challenges, even after most people have given up. Whether grit is a personality trait established early in life or a state that one can improve and develop has not yet been determined. It can be divided into two subsidiary aspects: consistency of interest and persistence of effort.

It appears that grit, unlike most personality traits, can be turned on or turned off—in other words, people may choose consciously when to express this behavior. Therefore, if we are interested in the impact of grit on job performance, we should study it by asking questions related to a workplace-specific context, whereas Duckworth's grit scale asks broad questions that could pertain to any part of life. To distinguish my use of grit from the broader use of the concept by Duckworth and others, I will refer to my construct as **Grit@Work**.

Psychological Capital

Yet another set of psychology concepts, described overall as psychological capital or PsyCap, evolved from the positive psychology movement pioneered by Martin Seligman. Positive psychology focuses on what people are doing right and on finding ways to improve how people think and the habits they create.

Fred Luthans, now retired after a 48-year career as a management professor at the University of Nebraska, popularized the concept of PsyCap (especially in his 2006 book *Psychological Capital: Developing the Human Competitive Advantage*) and became one of the world's most highly cited researchers. He and his colleagues claimed that the aspects of positive organizational behavior are "measurable, open to development, and can be managed for more effective work performance." Various studies have shown positive correlations between PsyCap and job performance in a wide range of business settings. Importantly, PsyCap is not a fixed trait; it can be developed over time.

In my research, I treated PsyCap as a *mediator*. That is a technical term in the social sciences, but I think I can explain it clearly with a simple analogy. If you have a traditional gas-powered car, it won't go anywhere unless you put fuel in it. The quality of the fuel affects how fast your car can go. However, the fuel has to go into an engine, which converts the fuel into the energy needed to move the car forward. Not all engines, of course, are the same. Your engine might work more or less efficiently depending on whether all its pistons are firing, or whether it is well oiled, or other factors. In that sense, the engine is a mediator that affects how well the fuel can cause your car to zoom down the highway.

In the same way, PsyCap is a mediator between personality traits and results. It is presumed to work as a motivational framework that affects how strongly other personality traits can impact job performance.

PsyCap is operationalized in terms of four sub-traits, which are easy to remember because they conveniently spell the acronym HERO.

Hope: This concept involves having "a will and a way"—that is, being determined to achieve a goal and having an idea of how to get there. Such a mental posture should certainly support professional achievement.

Efficacy: Efficacy means confidence that one can succeed. We develop efficacy over time through focused effort—attempting tasks, learning from our mistakes, and gradually gaining mastery, which reinforces confidence. A sense of efficacy has significant practical implications for performance in challenging situations.

Resiliency: This concept highlights the ability to "bounce back and beyond," in Luthans's words, or to overcome adversity and become strong, healthy, and successful again after something bad happens. It is particularly important in situations where disappointment and failure are common experiences.

Optimism: Seligman described optimism as a way in which people explain the world, or how they see and explain causes of bad events. Luthans added to this definition the idea of being realistic and flexible. A pie-in-the-sky type of unrealistic optimism is not usually helpful, but finding a way to take an optimistic view of a situation can prevent discouragement.

The four components of PsyCap may interrelate in ways that have not been fully comprehended, but it seems clear that PsyCap overall can make a powerful contribution to success.

Still More To Learn

By now, even if you had never heard of these psychological constructs previously, you can probably see how researchers could identify people with a strong likelihood of workplace success through personality studies. Indeed, a lot of this research exists. But no one had studied all these concepts in combination and how they relate to the performance of a relatively large number of highly successful salespeople. In that sense, my research was ground-breaking (after all, to earn a Ph.D. you are supposed to contribute new work that no one else has ever done before). In the next chapter, I briefly summarize what I did. After that, we will look at the results.

3

MY STUDY

To rigorously test the relationship between the personality variables discussed in the previous chapter and job performance, I needed to assemble a suitable set of measures and then have a sample of salespeople complete those measures so that I could analyze their responses. As you might expect, instruments to assess the HEXACO factors, grit, and PsyCap already existed. Since Grit@Work was an original invention, I had to develop a modified grit scale that concentrated solely on workplace issues.

I performed two preliminary studies. First, I validated the reliability of my Grit@Work scale by analyzing the answers given to each question. I tested 36 possible Grit@Work questions and retained 16 for the final study. I also tested job satisfaction as a proxy (i.e., a more convenient measure) for job performance and found that it was not reliable for this purpose. Accordingly, in the final study I made the extra effort to contact each participant's supervisor and request a confidential performance review of the employee.

For the actual study, I recruited 318 salespeople who worked in the insurance industry, either directly for insurance companies or for a software company that provides products to the insurance industry. Each salesperson was asked to complete a 148-item online survey that covered all the relevant personality variables, and the salesperson's supervisor was asked to complete a 24-item job performance scale. Given the large number of questions and the difficulty of obtaining and matching responses from both salespeople and their supervisors, I ended up with fully usable replies for 154 participants. All respondents were living in the United States (mostly in the Midwest), 82% of them were male, and their average salary was $137,358.

I then used high-level statistical analysis tools to examine the relationships between the variables. If you would like to check out the statistical methodology and the detailed results, they are all available in my dissertation.

4

THE FINDINGS

My analysis of the data revealed the following relationships:

- Extraversion was a predictor of psychological capital (in other words, salespeople who were high in extraversion also had high PsyCap).
- Grit was a predictor of PsyCap. However, if Grit was removed from the model, Conscientiousness provided similar predictive power as it relates to PsyCap.
- PsyCap was a strong predictor of job performance; salespeople with high PsyCap also had better performance ratings.
- Surprisingly, Openness to Experience was also significantly and *negatively* correlated with job performance. This relationship had not been found in previous research.

The discovery of the role of PsyCap was particularly exciting. My study marked the first research of this type with high-level business-to-business salespeople. The findings demonstrate the power of PsyCap in such an environment. This information greatly expands our ability to identify whom to hire or to predict how employees might perform in a sales setting. Moreover, it is valuable because we can increase employees' level of PsyCap through training interventions. (Please contact me if you would like information on the latest training available in this arena.)

I also analyzed the results for the other personality factors and constructed the following interpretations, which I think are quite credible based on my long experience with the world of insurance sales.

Honesty-Humility Matters

Depending on the culture and the products sold, Honesty-Humility certainly matters. In my overall dataset, Honesty-Humility was not a significant predictor of performance, because the different workplace cultures canceled each other out in the larger dataset. But when I looked at the data in a culture-specific manner, two things emerged. First, if you are selling a mix of property and casualty (i.e., B2B-related) products and personal lines, then high Honesty-Humility correlates with improved job performance. I believe that when one is selling personal lines, the consumer desires to work with someone who appears honest and trustworthy.

Alternatively, if you are the owner, operator, and top salesperson at a small to mid-sized insurance agency (or similar sales oriented business), you actually perform better if you are lower in Honesty-Humility. This situation appears to be connected with the dual role of the owner/salesperson, who needs to have a noticeable presence in the community. This presence sometimes requires lower levels of humility, so the person has to be somewhat comfortable engaging in self-promotion and perhaps even showing a few trappings of wealth, like a nice car or a Rolex watch.

Being low in Honesty-Humility does not necessarily mean that you are a dishonest person. A lower level of the personality trait of honesty may imply greater comfort with presenting information in the most favorable way possible so as to build relationships and close sales transactions. It is a fascinating phenomenon, but I don't interpret this as a negative. Obviously, there are some ethical lines that should not be crossed, but it is important to understand the subtle nuances and to recognize that you don't necessarily want the humblest, quietest, most squeaky-clean person running or owning your local agency or other type of B2B sales driven orgnaization.

Emotionality and Agreeableness

The traits of Emotionality and Agreeableness have not traditionally been shown to correlate with job performance in a sales environment. I agree that Emotionality and Agreeableness do not predict job performance in sales, because just about everyone who works in this field is agreeable and has high emotional control. In other words, if you are a stressed-out wreck and hard to get along with, you probably are not in a sales position. I am certain that these traits do matter, but if one does a research study on successful salespeople, those who are lower in these traits will not show up because they have already self-selected themselves out of the field.

The key question here is whether there are *variations* in these traits between salespeople that help us predict their job performance. I believe that using advanced modeling techniques can help us identify these differences and apply them in a predictive model.

Why Openness to Experience May Negatively Predict Performance

In my research data, Openness to Experience was a strong *negative* predictor of performance. This was not expected, but I believe I can make sense out of this unique finding.

Fifteen years ago, researchers Barbara Griffin and Beryl Hesketh investigated why Openness to Experience was the least useful trait in the personality models for predicting job performance. They concluded that Openness to Experience has two main foci, which they distinguished as openness to *internal* and *external* experience. In my study, the questions related to measuring openness to internal experience were significant negative predictors of performance. Griffin and Hesketh proposed that "perhaps people who are open to their internal states might have heightened awareness of negative feelings and, therefore, recognize or acknowledge degrees of anxiety." I suggest that this increased sense of self-awareness and perhaps greater sensitivity to anxiety, which are captured by questions on internal experience, lead to poorer performance in a sales environment. I believe that this is especially true in the high-dollar B2B sales environment that I studied. Although the research in this specific area is lacking,

I believe that this increased sensitivity leads to self-doubt, hesitation, and greater "call reluctance"—that is, internal resistance to making an initial sales call or to following up appropriately after an initial conversation.

A Grit Deficiency in the Younger Generation

As I looked at the levels of grit across all participants and ages, I noticed a gap between perseverance of effort (generally high) and consistency of interest (not so high) in younger salespeople. This difference narrowed in older salespeople. I call this the "video game effect." Real life doesn't give you a "treasure reward" every five minutes to keep your interest. Younger salespeople are able to persevere and work hard, but their consistency of interest jumps around too much. They may pursue a particular goal or new prospect for a period of time but quickly get frustrated, give up, and change the target of their perseverance to another goal. I have confirmed with some of the sales managers who participated in the study that they have also observed this phenomenon.

The solution is to make sales managers aware of this issue and to design performance metrics and rewards that reinforce the desirable long-term behaviors. Some sales managers have also implemented training programs to educate younger salespeople about this phenomenon and help them set appropriate expectations that encourage long-term consistency of interest.

PsyCap is HUGE!

I am a big booster of Psychological Capital as an identifier of effective employees and believe that its emergence as an influential factor in my study results is fully justified. First, at a conceptual level I believe in the power of hope, efficacy, resiliency, and optimism. Moreover, I believe you can effectively measure these traits in a person you are considering for a sales position. Also, as noted above, PsyCap is a malleable trait; if people don't already have a high level of PsyCap, you can nurture them in that direction, so I would encourage you to look for ways to increase the level of PsyCap among your sales team. You may be able find some training consultants locally who can assist you in this effort. If you are unable to locate an appropriate training organization, contact me for some recommendations.

Second, not only can you identify, through effective personality testing, those individuals who are high in Extraversion, but you can further differentiate which extraverts will be the best salespeople by also measuring their potential for PsyCap. Traditionally, Extraversion and Conscientiousness were pretty much the only traits you could look for when hiring salespeople. PsyCap adds a new effective dimension for fine-tuning your evaluation of candidates.

5

HOW YOU CAN USE THIS INFORMATION

My research originated from a very practical purpose: to improve our ability to identify people who have what it takes to succeed in sales, thereby resulting in better hiring results and happier employees. Accordingly, I will now give you a clear, simple set of practical guidelines on how to put these findings to work for your organization.

Use the MyPersonality® Assessment

I have developed a *free* personality assessment, called MyPersonality®, that incorporates my dissertation and additional subsequent research (explained further in the next chapter). The assessment is available in either of two ways:

- Visit DISCIPLINESTRATEGY.com and click on the MyPersonality page. Either you will see a free registration form to take the assessment or you will be asked for a code. The code, if requested, is **85285.** This version of the MyPersonality® assessment does NOT include the sales performance prediction report. (https://disciplinestrategy.com/my-personality/)

- If you are interested in the additional sales prediction report, it too is free. Visit SIGMAactuary.com, go to the education center page, and click the GET ACCESS NOW button. Register for free access to the educational portion of RISK66.com, which gives you access to the MyPersonality® assessment including the sales performance prediction report. (https://www.sigmaactuary.com/education-center/#signup)

Train Consistency of Effort

Train your younger salespeople in ways to stay on task and not to give up too soon on goal pursuits or prospects. Find ways to incentivize this behavior in your workplace.

Hire Extraversion and Conscientiousness

Use the MyPersonality® assessment as part of your screening process and hire people who score high in Extraversion and Conscientiousness.

Look for Perseverance

Hire people who show a commitment to perseverance. The MyPersonality® assessment measures perseverance from several different angles. You can also use interviewing techniques to assess this trait for yourself, asking candidates to discuss their personal history and describe situations in which they demonstrated perseverance.

Prioritize PsyCap

Hire people who have developed a positive psychological state. This characteristic can be probed during an interview. The MyPersonality® assessment (sales prediction version) also measures a person's capacity for PsyCap. Ideally, you want to find people who have high PsyCap and can maintain high intensity with low vulnerability to burnout. These characteristics are tested in the MyPersonality® assessment.

Be Flexible about Openness to Experience

Be careful with people high on the Openness to Experience scale. The results can be challenging to interpret. Some of the questions in the Openness to Experience scale do not measure the traits we are concerned about. You want to avoid hiring people who are highly aware of and sensitive to their internal state of being. These people may demonstrate some anxiety or exhibit high sensitivity to their feelings during the interview.

6

EXPANDING THE SCOPE: INCLUDING DISCIPLINE STRATEGY PSYCHOMETRICS TO CREATE THE MYPERSONALITY® ASSESSMENT

Around the time when I was finishing my dissertation research on personality factors, grit, PsyCap, and sales performance, I began working on my book DISCIPLINE STRATEGY (to be released in January 2020 by Forefront Books).

This research was designed to understand how personality traits can be used to better understand the driving components of personal success. I developed psychometrics (i.e., quantitative personality measurements) for each of 10 steps in the life change process, which I have named to create the acronym DISCIPLINE. See the graphic below for a summary of the 10 steps. Achieving significant goals, whether they are related to business or personal endeavors, involves a process that should ideally include each of these steps at least implicitly, even if a person does not consciously engage in each step explicitly and successively.

I combined my dissertation research and data with additional data gathering, interpretation, and adaptation of research results from a broad set of studies to create and validate metrics related to each of these steps. These metrics are incorporated, along with the testing of the personality factors described in the previous chapters of this booklet, in the MyPersonality® assessment, which also includes a projected sales performance metric.

All the measures are scored on a scale from 1 to 5 and are presented in a graphical format, compared to the average benchmark scores derived from an ever-growing pool of assessment takers. As of this writing, over 1,900 people have registered to take the MyPersonality® assessment. The explanatory report that is automatically and immediately generated when one completes the assessment defines the meaning of low and high values on each scale and presents text appropriate for the individual's own result on that scale, so as to assist with interpretation of the findings.

Following is a brief description of the 10 steps, accompanied by the questions associated with the assessment of an individual's ability to carry out each step effectively. Every question in this description has its own psychometric (a set of items within the

MyPersonality® inventory) designed to assess it. In some cases, I have provided additional explanatory information after the questions.

DECIDE (step 1)

Decision making involves several mental steps that are influenced by your personality and thought processes. Understanding your unique personality will help you make better and more informed decisions.

Q. Are you an organized decision maker who has self-discipline and deliberates on decisions with careful thought?

Q. As you are making your decision, are you open to new ideas, information, or pathways?

When you are approaching a big decision, I recommend that you put yourself into your "best mind" and take a calm approach to considering the options with open-mindedness. For some, this is an easy state to get into. For others, it can be hard to calm the sense of anxiety and be open to new possibilities. This measure shows your tendencies on an anxiety scale and an openness scale.

Knowing your tendencies will help you reserve the necessary time or effort to put yourself into your best mind, to be at peace, and to be open to new possibilities.

Q. Are you vulnerable to indecisiveness?

When faced with a decision or when simply wanting to make a life change, some people get stuck in the whirlwind of indecisiveness. This is something you will want to avoid.

Q. How much of a risk taker are you?

Some people are willing to tolerate more risk than others. This factor certainly affects the decisions you make. Knowing your risk tolerance may help you modify it consciously or motivate you to seek the opinions of others about your thoughts, plans, and decisions.

Q. Do you choke under pressure?

Your personality can help to predict whether your decision-making abilities will deteriorate or improve under pressure. Knowing this may help you plan the best time and conditions for your decision making. Items in the MyPersonality® assessment probe the quality of your decision making in both low-pressure and high-pressure contexts.

INVESTIGATE, SORT, CONCEIVE (steps 2 to 4)

Your performance in investigating and researching, sorting the information you find, and then conceiving a plan will be impacted by a set of personality sub-traits. The psychometrics below reflect scores on various traits that I have combined to create proprietary metrics, so as to help you anticipate challenges and compensate as needed.

Q. Will you be a good investigator as you gather information about your decision and build your knowledge base?

Some people love to research, dig into details, explore with a sense of curiosity, and push through the tedious process of digging up great information. Others struggle with this step in the process and may need help during the research phase. The relevant MyPersonality® metric shows what your personality predicts about your investigative ability, on a scale of low to high.

Q. How effective will you be in sorting and organizing all the information from your investigation to build your knowledge base?

Sorting and organizing information is a unique skill. It involves abstract reasoning, connecting the dots between a variety of information sources, focus, and perseverance. Some people enjoy this stage of the process, whereas others just sit and look at a pile of information and don't know what to do! The relevant MyPersonality® metric helps you identify whether this is a strength or a challenge for you.

Q. How effective will you be at conceiving a plan, based on your decision and knowledge base, that will provide a roadmap to your goal?

We all have our strengths and challenges. Conceiving a plan, after you have made a decision and conducted your research, is a uniquely challenging endeavor. Some people can combine several skills to conceive masterful plans. Others, even though they may have been great researchers, can't pull the pieces together to form a plan. This metric assesses how well you are suited for actually conceiving your plan.

IMPLEMENT, PERSEVERE, LOOP, INTENSIFY (steps 5 to 8)

Once you have conceived your plan, you are ready to implement it and fortify it so that you can persevere through challenges. After gaining some early experience, you will loop back in the process to tweak and improve your plan and methods. Then you will be ready for a period of intensity to push hard toward your goal. Your personality will influence how you handle each of these four steps.

Q. Will you effectively translate the plan you have conceived into an actionable roadmap that you will implement effectively?

Transitioning to implementation is a difficult point for many people. Deciding, investigating, sorting, and conceiving a plan are predominantly mental activities. Implementation requires you to start actually doing—acting, moving, and choosing to do what you have decided to do on a daily basis. Your personality can serve you well or hold you back at this stage of the process.

Q. What is your capacity for perseverance and grit?

This is a measure of your capacity to persevere in the face of challenges and display grit when necessary or motivated. Ideally, the decision you have made and the path you are on will bring out your highest level of determination.

Q. What is your vulnerability to burnout?

Burnout is a serious concern for many people. A period of intense, highly focused work can lead to mental and physical exhaustion, a decrease in emotional connections with work and people, and reduced performance. Knowing your vulnerability to burnout will inform how hard you can push and how often you may need to recharge.

Q. What is your capacity for intensity?

Capacity for intensity would seem to be the opposite of vulnerability to burnout, but that is not always the case. Some people have neither tendency—that is, they are not at risk of burning out but neither are they capable of intense effort. It is important to view these two metrics together. Capacity for intensity represents your ability to engage with intense focus and effort in achieving your plan and pursuing a goal.

PREDICTING SALES PERFORMANCE

The final page of the MyPersonality® assessment report uses proprietary models to generate two psychometrics: capacity for Psychological Capital and capacity for sales job performance.

Capacity for Psychological Capital. Although psychological capital is a strong predictor of sales performance, the *capacity* for psychological capital is a better representation of a candidate's potential sales performance, because psychological capital is a malleable state that can be influenced through training and by the surrounding environment. Don't give up on someone who may not have much PsyCap now but whose personality testing evidences the capacity to develop it.

Capacity for Sales Job Performance. This metric combines my proprietary research database of high-performing sales people, derived from my dissertation research, with my subsequent additional research on personality traits. The development of this metric was also influenced by research into the various DISCIPLINE process steps and by third-party studies.

Finally, an overall sales performance recommendation is presented on a scale from 1 to 5. It incorporates both capacity for PsyCap and capacity for sales job performance.

The Full Picture

I believe that the MyPersonality® assessment is uniquely valuable because it gives you a broader portrait of a candidate than any other instrument. It includes a pure sales performance prediction tool as its final metric, and in addition, the full personality profile (six main traits and 24 sub-traits) and the DISCIPLINE process psychometrics help you understand more fully how this person will perform and where he or she is likely to encounter challenges. Even if you use other assessment tools, I encourage you to add the MyPersonality® assessment to your toolkit to gain a more complete picture.

7

CONCLUSION

This research has been eye-opening and exciting, but ironically, it confirmed some of my natural intuitions from my days as a young entrepreneur.

At age 26, I started my first business, a software company. I often worked 18-hour days, sometimes seven days a week. I had two posters that hung on my office wall. One said "Perseverance" and the other said "Your Attitude Determines Your Altitude."

Now, 29 years later—having supported thousands of great salespeople, completed a Ph.D. program, and studied the personalities of the best salespeople in the country—I find the wisdom from those two posters to be true. Much of one's success, whether as a salesperson or in the pursuit of a goal, depends on having a combination of positivity (Psychological Capital) and perseverance.

A new generation of advanced analytical models is just now starting to impact personality modeling and hiring. These models will eventually help companies make better hires and help individuals to better understand themselves so that they can increase the likelihood of reaching a significant life goal. Hiring great salespeople will become easier, and I believe that MyPersonality® is a big step in that direction.

I hope you will enjoy and benefit from the MyPersonality® assessment as my gift to the greatest profession in the world: sales. I also hope that you will check out my book DISCIPLINE STRATEGY, available in January 2020.

Visit my website at: https://disciplinestrategy.com/

REFERENCES

(You can find a complete list of more than 100 references to relevant research in my dissertation. This reference list contains only the sources quoted directly in this booklet and those that I would strongly recommend for further reading.)

Ashton, M. C., Lee, K., et al. (2004). A six-factor structure of personality-descriptive adjectives: Solutions from psycholexical studies in seven languages. *Journal of Personality and Social Psychology, 86*(2), 356–366. (This is Ashton and Lee's paper introducing Honesty-Humility as a sixth personality factor.)

Buchanan, G. M., & Seligman, M. E. P. (Eds.). (1995). *Explanatory style.* Hillsdale, NJ: Lawrence Erlbaum. (This edited volume captures part of Martin Seligman's influence by collecting papers on how people tend to explain events—e.g., whether they view events in an optimistic or pessimistic way.)

Duckworth, A. L., Peterson, C., Matthews, M. D., & Kelly, D. R. (2007). Grit: perseverance and passion for long-term goals. *Journal of Personality and Social Psychology, 92*(6), 1087–1101. (The original paper that introduced the concept of grit.)

Duckworth, A. (2016). *Grit: The power of passion and perseverance.* New York: Scribner.

Griffin, B., and Hesketh, B. (2004). Why openness to experience is not a good predictor of job performance. *International Journal of Selection and Assessment, 12*(3), 243–251.

Johnson, M. K., Rowatt, W. C., & Petrini, L. (2011). A new trait on the market: Honesty–Humility as a unique predictor of job performance ratings. *Personality and Individual Differences, 50*(6), 857-862. (This study provides the evidence for my statement in chapter 2, "Honesty-Humility has also been shown to be a predictor of job performance even when controlling for Conscientiousness.")

Lee, K., & Ashton, M. C. (2004). Psychometric properties of the HEXACO Personality Inventory. *Multivariate Behavioral Research, 39*(2), 329–358.

Luthans, F., Luthans, K. W., & Luthans, B. C. (2004). Positive psychological capital: Beyond human and social capital. *Business Horizons,*

47(1), 45–50. (The quotation in the explanation of PsyCap in chapter 2 comes from this article.)

Luthans, F., Youssef, C. M., & Avolio, B. J. (2006). *Psychological capital: Developing the human competitive edge.* Oxford: Oxford University Press. (Fred Luthans's popular-level work on PsyCap.)

Norman, W. T. (1963). Toward an adequate taxonomy of personality attributes: Replicated factor structure in peer nomination personality ratings. *Journal of Abnormal and Social Psychology*, *66*(6), 574–583. (One of the early studies that postulated the Big Five personality model.)

Vinchur, A. J., Schippmann, J. S., Switzer III, F. S., & Roth, P. L. (1998). A meta-analytic review of predictors of job performance for salespeople. *Journal of Applied Psychology*, *83*(4), 586–597. (An excellent summary of the results of studies on salespeople up through 1998.)